I0494163

First Time Home Buyer Guidance

...From an Expert Agent

Gena Martin
Copyright Gena Martin 2014

Table of Contents

Acknowledgments

First and foremost, I would like to thank my husband Jay Martin for standing beside me and pushing me throughout my life, career, and the writing of this guide. He has been my guide, my inspiration, and motivation for continuing to improve my life and move my career beyond what I thought possible. He is my rock and I accomplish much because of him. I also thank my three awesomazing children: Haley, Jayme, and Wyatt for understanding all the time I put into meeting my goals and growing my businesses. Finally, thanks to my parents, Eugene and Jackie Young, who taught me to exhibit good work ethic and responsibility.

Having a place to live is home.
Having someone to live with is family.
Having both is a wonderful life
....Ali Bassam

Introduction

Home ownership is probably one of the biggest things people work for today. People want the stability of owning their own home. However, buying your first home can be an overwhelming journey for any buyer. Not only are you making one of the most important purchases of your life, the whole process of figuring your finances, qualifying for a mortgage, finding an expert real estate agent, deciding on the right house, working through negotiations, signing of contracts, and closing the deal – can be intimidating to even the shrewdest buyer.

As a real estate investor and an expert real estate agent, I have written this guide to help demystify the home buying process. The information in this guide will help you to decide if you are ready to buy a home, inform you of what you'll need to do before you start hunting for a home, and what you can expect from the buying process itself.

Please read on and use this guide to help you through the process of buying your first home.

"Owning a home is the culmination of many years of hard work and the realization of the American Dream."
~ Solomon Ortiz

Are You Ready?

Figuring out if you are even ready to take real steps to buying your first home starts here. This stage should be done on your own and maybe with the help of family members. Planning is one of the steps to making the home buying process easier. If after doing this preliminary work you find that your finances and/or credit history is less than shiny, you're probably better off renting while you take the necessary steps to polish everything up.

1) Do you know where you are financially?
Having a clear understanding of your financial situation is extremely important when you are considering buying a home. Begin by preparing a financial statement, figuring out how much money you have coming in and going out each month. This process will help you to figure out how much you can afford to spend on a new home. *See the GMR financial statement worksheet in the back of this book.

Remember that a new home comes with more expenses. What is the average home price in your area? Use this number to make a mock budget. Add up what your new mortgage payment would be, property taxes, homeowners insurance, and home maintenance/upkeep costs. If you can't afford these extra expenses, it is never a good time to buy, no matter what the market says.

Do you have toxic debt; loans of which you are either unwilling or unable to make payments? This is a sign that you are probably already living beyond your means or spending more money than you make. You need to wipe away any/all toxic debt that you may have. If you don't get your overspending under control before you buy a home, your problems are likely to get much worse, since home ownership comes with plenty of other costs.

2) Do you have a good credit score and a sizable down payment?

You don't have to have a perfect credit history to purchase a home, but a good history can mean paying less for your home. A low credit score results in high interest rates and a high credit score will have the lender offering you the lowest interest rates possible. If you don't have a credit history, you will need to work on getting some. However, if you have credit cards or student loans, your probably already on track.

Your credit history is available to you for free, once per year, from each of the three main credit bureaus at annualcreditreport.com. Checking your report for errors is a good idea, since they can eliminate your chances of obtaining a loan or cause you to have to pay higher interest rates.

Lenders like to see a borrower with some personal stake in the deal. Make sure you have enough money set aside for a down payment and any additional costs you will incur when buying a home such as a home inspection fee, closing costs, title insurance fee, etc. *Conventional loans* are going to require 10 percent to 20 percent down payment, varying by lender and location. If you can reach the 20% level, you can avoid paying PMI (private mortgage insurance) plus you will have more equity, which helps your credit score and acts as an asset on your balance sheet that you can borrow against (if you qualify) when you need the money.

FHA loans have surged in popularity, largely because of the low down payment (3.5% minimum) and credit score requirements (580). Some lenders offer FHA programs for lower scores (between 500-579) with a 10% down payment. FHA loans tend to come with lower interest rates as well. So if you have a less then satisfactory credit history and/or don't like the idea of a 20% down payment, this may be a good option for you.
*Keep in mind of the downfall of an FHA loan, which is the mortgage insurance requirement that is, many times, for the life of the loan.

The USDA first time home buyer loan allows a borrower to finance an amount up to 100% of the properties total value upon appraisal. The borrower can also factor repair and renovation costs into the loan. Mortgage insurance is not a loan requirement, therefore allowing the borrower with a less than perfect credit score, the ability to qualify.

If your a Veteran you can take advantage of the *VA loan program*. Another loan program allowing a borrower to finance up to 100% of the homes value and purchase with no money down. Because the loan is backed by the government, there is no PMI (private mortgage insurance) requirement.

Don't be overwhelmed by the amount of loan programs available. Your loan officer will help you decide what program is best for you. Note: This service should be at no cost to you.

3) Do you have a reliable income?
You will need to show a steady source of reliable income and that you have been employed on a regular basis, preferably at the same place, for the last 2-3 years. With a new home comes a long term financial commitment and extra expenses that come with home ownership.

4) Are your debts under control?
Lenders are going to make sure your debt is at a manageable level. They will be looking at your debt-to-income ratio, to examine whether your monthly housing costs - including principal, interest, taxes, and insurance- consume no more than the "preferred" 28% of your monthly gross income and that your total minimum debt payments including your mortgage, car payments, credit cards, and installment loans will remain below the "preferred" 36% of your gross pay. That's why if you have large outstanding debts, it is a good idea to pay them down prior to applying for a mortgage.

You will find less rigid guidelines for people with stellar credit and/or a large down payment. Guidelines vary according to loan program- FHA guidelines state a 29/41 qualifying ratio as acceptable. VA guidelines have no front ratio, yet the guideline for the back ratio is 41.

5) Do you know what you want?

So you've done a personal financial statement, checked over your credit reports, and feel that you have plenty of money to put towards buying a new home. Your next step is deciding what kind of home you want.

Although it is important to know how many bedrooms and/or bathrooms you want and whether you want a garage or not, there are other things that first time home buyers overlook that are far more important. Such as...

Choosing the right neighborhood.
At some point you will probably want to or need to sell your home. It is important that you choose the right neighborhood when you purchase your home, so that down the road you will be rewarded with a higher valued home that will be easy to sell.

Is the home located in a good school district?
Are there popular school districts in your area? Even if you don't have kids yet, buying a home within that school district will make your home more appealing to buyers who may want to purchase your home in the future.

How are the neighbors?
Don't just look at the home you are interested in buying. Be sure to check out the neighboring homes as well. Nobody wants to live next to an eyesore or kept awake all night due to a loud neighbor. Do a little homework. Talk to the neighbors or drive through the neighborhood at different hours of the day to see what is going on and/or who's out and about.

Most first time home buyers tend to be a little enthusiastic at the start of their home search. It is important that you, as a first time home buyer, make choices that stay within your budget. Avoid luxuries that you cannot yet afford. Your next step, the pre-approval process, will let you know just how much you can afford, which will help you to narrow down your home choices in a market with an average to large inventory.

"In dreams begin responsibilities." ~ *W.B. Yeats*

Your First Move, "The Pre-Approval"

It is important before you start searching for a home to get a pre-approval letter. This should be your first stop in the home buying process. It is fast, free, and easy. Why is this first move so important?...

1) Figuring out how much money you qualify to borrow. Most buyers have a good idea of what they are comfortable paying out each month on their mortgage. However, it is very important to calculate other factors in such as down payment percentage, interest rates, mortgage insurance, property taxes, property insurance, and so on. Also, depending on your credit history, your income, and your debts, you may find out that you don't qualify to borrow as much as you thought. Save yourself the grief of falling in love with a home you can't afford.

2) You will have more leverage when time to negotiate with a seller. Sellers want real estate agents to bring pre-approved buyers to their homes. They don't want to waste their time staging and leaving their home for you to tour, only to find out later that you hadn't even been to a lender yet. Sellers want to know that the buyer has been financially qualified to acquire the financing they need to close a transaction. A pre-approval letter could also be in your favor in a close multiple offer situation. The ability to send in a pre-approval letter along with your offer, is an additional benefit in helping you acquire your dream home.

3) Your real estate agent will take you serious and work hard for you. Believe it or not, some agents will not show properties to buyers without a pre-approval letter and some sellers don't want agents showing their homes to buyers that are not pre-approved. Your pre-approval letter indicates to the agent and seller, that you are a well qualified buyer and that you're serious about purchasing a home. The probability of a completed transaction will inspire your agent to apply more time and the get-up-and-go to your home search.

**FYI, there should not be a charge for obtaining a pre-approval letter.

"Luck is what happens when preparation meets opportunity." ~ Seneca

Finding an Expert Real Estate Agent

Finding an expert real estate agent is important, but beware, not all real estate agents are created equal! Selling real estate is hard work! Roughly seventy percent of agents quit within their first year and out of those who make it through their first year, around eighty percent of those quit within the next 5 years. This professional will be leading you in every aspect of the home buying process, and so choosing the right one can mean the difference between failure and success for you.

Some tips on finding an expert....

Referrals: Asking your family, friends, neighbors, and/or co-workers, is the most common way of finding an expert agent. However, make sure they actually did their homework, by asking them how they went about qualifying their agent. What was their experience with this agent? Due to the fact that most people will not do the work to get those details, make sure you do.

Search Work: Search for local expert agents with recommendations and/or testimonials from past home buyers. You may find that online agents may be referred to you on certain websites, but it has no value. Just like the newspapers, unless an agent has some kind of feature story, they can simply buy ad space. Again, no merit of the quality of the agent.

Expert agents should have recommendations that can be seen on the internet or have them available upon request.

Interview: It is important to talk to or research the agent. Ask them questions or find the answers.

Do you have a media page or resume?
This should show their past/present experiences. Any agent with this on site is ahead of the game. An expert agent uses this as an opportunity to display experience, recognitions, accomplishments, and expertise.

What technology do you use as an agent?
An expert agent will be out in their work environment and spends very little time at their desk. An expert agent will be plugged into the internet, by laptop, desktop, and mobile...which are all requirements for efficient and instant access. Look for an agent who is internet and technology savvy. Since 90% of all home searches begin online, you'll want an agent who knows how to search and market homes online. Also, in this time of popular social media outlets, expert agents should have a good following and connections on basic sites such as Facebook, Twitter, and LinkedIn (online sites where you can easily research a tech savvy expert agent and their experiences).

How many clients do you currently represent?
Agents with to many listings or to many sales, may seem like the go to agent, but may have more than they can handle. That's not to say that the agent is not a good agent, however if you are looking for personal, one-on-one collaboration with the agent you do hire, don't hire the agent with to much. The more clients an agent represents, the thinner his/her attention is spread. If you suddenly find a home online, you will want an agent who is quick to move and can accommodate your last minute showing needs.

How does the agent serve his/her clients?
You should find a real estate expert that you feel comfortable with and that you can easily talk with. Make sure the real estate expert you choose displays a positive attitude and shows you that they will do everything in your best interest. You will also want a real estate expert who shows that they can take the lead and be aggressive in making things happen.

Is the agent to busy?
I'll be the first to admit that you want a strong, hard-working, go-getter of an agent working for you! On the other hand, you don't want an agent that is to busy. An expert agent can work effectively with about a half-dozen buyers at any one time while continuing to give the time needed to a buyer. If they have to many more than that, you may not get the personnel attention that you desire.

In the end, it is definitely worth some extra time and effort to find an expert agent who's personality, drive, experience and skill level meets your needs and makes you even more excited about the home-buying process.

"If you think it's expensive to hire a professional to do the job, wait until you hire an amateur."
~ Red Adair

Meeting Your Expert Agent

After you have chosen which expert agent will assist you in the home-buying process, you will then set up a day and time to meet with the agent about getting started.

At this first meeting, you will bring along your pre-approval letter and be ready to discuss with the agent the kind of home you are looking for. Since 90% of buyers begin their home search online, there is a chance you have already found homes that you would like to tour. It is a good idea to bring that information to the meeting as well.

Having a list is helpful. What does your dream home look like? Does it have a porch? How many bedrooms and bathrooms will you need? How much space do you desire? What kinds of things do you want in your kitchen? Does it have appliances? Do you need lots of storage? Do you need a garage or a basement? Think about the type of yard that you want. Do you need a big yard? Do you need it fenced in for your kids or pets? Do you need outbuildings?

After you have made a list of the things you want or need in a house, think bout the type of neighborhood you want to live in. If you have children, it may be important that you locate a house in a specific school district. What about your commute to and from work? Also, you will want to make sure you purchase a home in an area that has a good rate of home appreciation or will at least retain its value.

A good agent will help you to focus on things you really need, since they know that many first time home-buyers do not get everything on their "wish-list" in their first home.

By the end of this first meeting, the agent should have gathered all the information needed to begin the hunt for a home.

"Failing to set goals is like setting out on a road trip without a map." —Michelle Moore

The Hunt

An expert agent will have listened to your wants and needs and will arrange to show you only homes that are very close to what you are looking for. This will save the agent and the buyer from wasting valuable time. It is not a good idea to tour more than three to five homes per meet-up, since touring any more than that can become overwhelming to the buyer.

When touring a home, feel free to turn on lights, look in pantry's, open doors and closets and all the things that allow you to ensure the home is right for you. Your agent will be along side you making sure to re-secure the home after the tour.

Be sure to ask your agent any questions that come to you while touring each home. If the agent does not know the answer, he/she should be able to get the answer for you.

Motivated buyers will usually find a home within a couple of weeks, however, sometimes finding the right property can take time. It is important to stay motivated and not get discouraged if you don't find something right away.

You can't always get what you want.
But if you try, sometimes you just might find you get
what you need...Rolling Stones

Offers-Negotiations-Contracts

Congratulations! You have found your dream home and you are ready to make an offer.

Expert real estate agents are invaluable when it comes time to make an offer on a house!
There are many different and important pieces to completing this process with success. No way is the right way and every transaction is different.
Negotiating begins with the first offer and will continue on, until an agreement is made between the seller and the buyer. Sometimes a seller and buyer cannot come to an agreement and the offer will die.

Your initial offer is usually lower than the asking price of the home. The first offer is also your opportunity to gather information about the sellers true motivation for selling.

Keep in mind, if houses are selling quickly and many houses are receiving multiple offers, you'll need to bid competitively. However, if homes are on the market in your area for a longer period of time then you may have a bit more wiggle room for negotiating. A good offer will contain a few basic elements.

 ⅄   Your offer should be realistic. It is not normally a good idea to offer $20,000 less than the asking price of a home. Base your offer on comparable homes in the area that have SOLD in the last six months, if possible. Use homes of the same size, with the same features, and in the same condition of the home you are going to be putting an offer on. Your real estate agent should be able to help you with this.

A   Your pre-approval letter will indicate to the seller that you are serious, so be sure to let them know in the offer that you are pre-approved for financing. This is where you will have the advantage over someone who has not yet done the work of getting their financing ready before hand. Make sure your financing terms are reasonable and up-to-date.

A   Be sure to use the property inspection clause. This will allow you to reopen negotiations in the event that problems arise. There may be property defects that you nor the seller are aware of. What if it is determined that the heating and cooling system is faulty or the roof needs replaced? These types of repairs could cost a few thousand dollars. It is a good idea to have a property inspected by a licensed home inspector. Using the property inspection clause will allow a buyer to renegotiate the price and/or repairs if corrective work is needed.

A   It is important to include Conveyances. This includes what is included in the sale. For instance, a refrigerator, electric range, and a microwave. You want to make sure to add what you expect to be included in the sale of the home your are buying on the contract.

- The amount of your earnest money deposit. The earnest money deposit can range from $500 to 3% of the value of the home. This deposit is typically put towards your closing costs; however, if you enter into a contract with the seller and then breach that contract, you could lose this money.

- An expiration date, by which the seller must respond or your offer expires.
Two days (48 hours) is usually a good time frame.

Make sure everything is in writing. If the sellers have verbally indicated that they will give you a carpet allowance but it is not written in the offer, then you may not get the money.

Once you make a purchase offer, sign it, and submit it to the seller (this is usually done through your agent), the seller has the right to sign your offer as is, make a counter offer, or reject your offer outright.

If the seller accepts your purchase offer, the offer becomes a contract, and you are on your way to owning the home. If the seller counters your offer, you may choose to counter back on his or her offer, or you may walk away.

This all my seem overwhelming, but an expert agent will be able to lead you through the entire process.

"The most important trip you may take in life is meeting people half way." – Henry Boyle

The Closing

After weeks or maybe months of working alongside your agent and mortgage officer, the big day has come! Closing Day! The day you get to seal the deal and gain ownership of your first home! This usually takes place at a local title company office. This process will usually take an hour to an hour and a half and involves the signing of legal documents and paying closing costs.

The closing is a term used for the point in time at which the title to the property is transferred to the buyer and, generally, a mortgage or "deed of trust" is given by the buyer/borrower to the lender.

Who is usually at the closing? The closing agent, you and anyone else that will be on the property title, your real estate agent, the home seller, the home sellers agent, and your lender are usually present at closing.

Your agent will have preliminary title work ordered. A title professional will then search and examine public records for all information related to the home's title. This will provide any information of flaws on a property such as liens, judgments, or unpaid taxes. Title Companies work hard to make sure any issues with a property will be dealt with and satisfied before you go to close on the property.

Finally, a settlement agent will prepare a HUD-1 settlement statement. This statement will outline all the costs for both the buyer and seller associated with the closing.

Closing day the property will be transferred from the seller to the buyer. Once the signing of all legal documents is complete and closing costs are paid, the house is yours! Go home and start packing.

You should know that after the home is yours, the seller, under normal circumstances, will have 30 days to move out of the home. So unless the home is vacant and/or you negotiated possession under different terms, you will have to wait to take possession of your new home.

There is no such thing as the perfect home,
but there is a home that is perfect for you
...Sheena Weatherly

First Time Home-buyers Frequently Asked Questions

Where do I begin?

You start by getting a pre-approval from a lender. You need to determine how much you can spend on a home before you begin hunting for a home. If you don't know a good lender, choose your expert agent first and he/she can recommend good lenders to you. Don't take the chance of losing your dream home! Be ready to buy by being pre-approved before you start looking.

Should I buy or rent?

The drive to be a homeowner is strong. It's mostly about freedom and being able to do what you want to do. However, whether you should buy or rent is going to depend on your financial situation and the current market in your area. Although buying a home gives you a greater amount of freedom to do what you want with it, it also comes with greater responsibilities such as maintenance, taxes, and insurance. Your lender can help you determine if buying a home is in your best interest.

Why should I use a Realtor?

For most people, buying a home is the most expensive purchase they will make in their lifetime. It's a serious transaction with emotional and financial ramifications for the parties involved and having expert representation is very important. Not only does a Realtor have all the tools at their fingertips to help you find the right home, but they also keep up with the ever-changing regulations, know how to figure the value of a home, the negotiation process, legal documents, and how to follow the code of ethics. Realtor representation in a real estate transaction is very important for both the buyer and the seller. The real question should be, "Why would you not use the free services of a professional who's career is focused on helping people to locate their dream home?"

How much money will I have to come up with to buy a home?

That depends on things such as; the home you are buying and the type of mortgage you are using. Usually you will have to come up with enough money for three things: earnest money – the deposit you make when you submit an offer on a home, to prove to the seller that you are serious about buying their home; the down payment – a percentage of the cost of your home that you must pay depending on your mortgage type; and the closing costs – the costs associated with processing the paperwork involved in buying a home.

What other costs are associated with owning a home?

Buying a home involves other costs in addition to your new monthly mortgage payment. You will have to take care of the upkeep and maintenance, pay the property taxes, keep the home insured, pay utilities, and furnish your home.

How long does it take to buy a home?

After writing up a contract, it typically takes from 30 – 45 days to close. The time it takes to get possession of your new home will depend on what you negotiated in your contract, normally 30 days after closing. It is a good idea to start your hunt about 3 months before you actually want to be in possession of your new home.

Can you recommend service providers who can help me obtain a mortgage, make home repairs, and help with other things I need done?

A good agent will have a team of professionals in your area that they can recommend for services that you may be in need of.

Can I become a home buyer if I have had bad credit and I don't have a large enough down payment?

Yes, talk to your agent about buying a home on contract, sometimes called contracts for deed.

A land contract bypasses a conventional lender. The buyer makes a small down payment and monthly payments directly to the seller at an agreed-upon interest rate and time period. The contract typically runs two or three years, at which time the buyer should be able to qualify for conventional financing and pay off the balance.

Do I need to get a Home Inspection?

It is highly recommended that you always get an inspection on a home before you buy it. If the home has major repairs needed, you will want to be able to negotiate a lower price for the home or the repairs to be fixed. If the problems are to big or unsettling, you will want to be able to opt-out of buying the home. A home inspection is vital for buyers and and the cost is usually just a few hundred bucks — well worth it to provide peace of mind and to know that your not getting yourself into a financial mess!

A home inspection is an important part of your home buying process, to determine if further negotiations are necessary, to save you from hidden costly repairs
....Gena Martin Realtor

About the Author

Gena Martin has been an avid entrepreneur since the age of 25. Along with her husband, they have developed many businesses from the ground up. Businesses from sports entertainment and landscaping to investments and real estate. Gena started her real estate career as an investor, when her and her husband purchased their first 3 bedroom/1 bath foreclosed home in Kokomo, Indiana. She currently sales residential and commercial real estate in Indiana and continues to help manage her other existing businesses. Gena is recognized as an expert author and columnists in real estate. She was recently featured on TLC Network. When she's not selling real estate, shes probably working out, gardening, cooking, or writing. Gena and her husband, Jay, have been married for 25 years. They have three grown children – Haley, Jayme, and Wyatt.

Real Estate Articles/Videos By Gena Martin

Articles

http://www.i-newswire.com/why-consumers-should-make-the-move/210932

http://ezinearticles.com/?Should-You-Sell-or-Keep-Betting-the-Farm?&id=7531612

http://www.i-newswire.com/risky-business-by-gena-martin/244516

http://www.inewswire.com/real-estates-largest-overlooked/257814

Videos

Featured on TLC Network:

https://www.youtube.com/watch?v=T930VaGKkUM

Connect With Gena Martin

I really appreciate you reading my book! Here are my social media coordinates:

Friend me on Facebook:
https://www.facebook.com/GenaMartinRealtor
Follow me on Twitter:
https://twitter.com/MovewithMartin
Connect on LinkedIn:
https://www.linkedin.com/in/genamartinrealtor
Visit my website: www.genamartinrealtor.com
Join my Circle: google.com/+GenaMartin

Seek out an expert agent by reviewing their referrals, social media pages, and even a google search. This can help determine how active the agent is in their field of expertise...Gena Martin Realtor

GMR **Personal Financial Statement**

Name: _____

Monthly Gross Income	
Borrower	
Co-Borrower	
Net Sales	

Monthly Net Income	
Borrower	
Co-Borrower	
Social Security	
Pension	
Child Support	
Other Income	
Other Income	
Total Net Income	

Expenses			
1st Mortgage		Credit Card #3	
2nd Mortgage / Contract for Deed		Credit card #4	
Property Taxes (if not Escrow)		Student Loans	
Association Dues		Chapter 13 Trustee Payments	
House Insurance (if not Escrow)		Work Related Expenses	
Heat/Gas		School Lunches	
Electricity		Educational expenses	
Telephone		Pet Food /Vet Care/ Grooming	
Pager/Cell Phone		Dry Cleaning and Laundry	
Water/Sewer		Household Supplies	
Trash		Clothing	
Home Repairs and Maintenance		Personal Care Items	
Food and Groceries		Beauty Shop/Barber	
Automobile Payment		Gifts/Presents	
Gasoline for Automobile		Entertainment/Eating Out	
Automobile Insurance		Cable TV	
Automobile Repairs and Maintenance		Donations/Tithings	
Bus fare		Cigarettes/Alcohol	
Alimony/Child Support		Savings account	
Child Care		Life Insurance	
Credit Card #1		Doctor/ Dentist/ Rx/ Glasses	
Credit Card #2		Other:	

Total Expense

Household Balance